M

Ma~~~ ~~~

The Story of Moses
Accurately retold from the Bible
(from the books of Exodus, Leviticus,
Numbers and Deuteronomy),
by Carine Mackenzie

Illustrations by Duncan McLaren
Cover design by Daniel van Straaten

Copyright © 2008 Carine Mackenzie
ISBN 978-1-84550-381-9
Reprinted 2012 and 2021
Published by
Christian Focus Publications,
Geanies House, Fearn, Tain, Ross-shire, IV20 1TW, Scotland.
www.christianfocus.com
Printed by Veritas Press

The Hebrew people had become slaves in Egypt. They were cruelly treated and had to do hard back-breaking work, making bricks. Pharaoh the king gave orders to kill all the baby boys born to the Hebrew families.

Amram and Jochebed lived in Egypt with their son Aaron and daughter Miriam. A baby boy was born to that Hebrew family. His mother was able to hide him for three months but as he grew older it became difficult to keep him quiet.

Jochebed made a basket of bulrushes which she covered with tar to keep it water-tight. She placed her baby in the basket and floated it in the reeds by the banks of the River Nile. Big sister Miriam watched to see what would happen.

Pharaoh's daughter came down to the river to bathe. She noticed the basket among the reeds and ordered her maid to fetch it. She took pity on the baby and decided to adopt him. She called him Moses which means 'drawn out of the water'.

Miriam stepped up to offer to find a nurse for the princess and so Jochebed was given that job and was able to look after her baby openly.

When Moses was old enough he went to live in the royal palace as the son of Pharaoh's daughter – a very important position. Even in this wealthy life-style Moses never forgot that he belonged to the Hebrew people. He worshipped the one true God as his parents would have taught him.

One day Moses saw an Egyptian beating a Hebrew slave. This made him very angry. He killed the Egyptian and buried his body in the sand when no one was looking. The next day when he tried to stop two Hebrew men fighting, one accused him. 'Are you going to kill me like you killed the Egyptian?'

Moses' action was not a secret. Pharaoh was furious. Moses was scared. He left Egypt and hid in the land of Midian many miles away.

Moses spent forty years in Midian. He got married and had two sons. He looked after his father-in-law's sheep in the desert. One day he saw something very strange – a bush was on fire but was not being burnt up.

God spoke to Moses from the bush. 'Take off your shoes; you are standing on holy ground.' God told Moses that he saw how badly treated his people were in Egypt. 'I will rescue them. I want you to speak to Pharaoh, and lead my people out of Egypt.'

Moses was afraid of such a big task, but God promised to help him.

God has made many promises to us too. He speaks to us in his Word the Bible. He has promised never to leave those who trust in him.

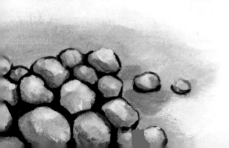

Moses and Aaron, his brother, went to speak to Pharaoh. 'Let my people go,' they asked. Pharaoh refused. He made the work of the Hebrew slaves even harder. They had to gather straw themselves and still make the same number of bricks.

God sent plagues to the land of Egypt as a punishment to Pharaoh. The water of the river Nile was turned to blood. Hundreds of frogs swarmed over the land – even into the houses, into the beds and cupboards. Still Pharaoh would not let the people go.

God sent lice, flies, cattle disease, boils, hail, locusts and darkness.

Pharaoh still had a hard heart.

The final plague was the worst of all. 'Then Pharaoh will let you go,' God told Moses. Moses warned Pharaoh, 'At midnight every first born child in every family will die.'

The Hebrew families would escape. Moses passed on God's instructions. The best lamb of the flock was to be killed; the blood painted on the door posts and lintels of the house. When the angel of death passed through Egypt he would pass over the houses marked with the blood.

The people ate a special meal of roast lamb with herbs and unleavened bread. Every Egyptian family was affected by death.

At last Pharaoh changed his mind. 'Go and serve the Lord,' he said. 'Take your flocks and herds too.'

God saved his people from slavery. God has a wonderful plan to save his people from the slavery to sin. The blood of the Lord Jesus Christ was shed to make sure that those who trust in him would have eternal life.

God's people escaped from Egypt. When they reached the Red Sea they felt trapped – sea in front and soldiers behind. Moses encouraged them, 'Do not be afraid,' he said. 'Stand firm and see the salvation of the Lord.'

God told Moses to hold out his staff over the Red Sea. God drove the sea back by a strong east wind. Moses led the people across a clear path to the other side.

When the Egyptian soldiers followed, the chariot wheels stuck. God told Moses to stretch out his hand over the sea again. The waves came flooding back, drowning the Egyptians.

The people saw God's power and believed in him.

Soon the people started to complain. 'We used to have plenty to eat in Egypt,' they moaned. 'Now we are so hungry.' God heard them and provided. That evening the camp was covered with birds called quails. That gave them plenty of meat to eat.

God provided bread too. In the morning the ground was covered with little white seeds called manna. Each family collected what they needed for the day. On the sixth day of the week they collected twice as much, some to use on the Sabbath because God did not send manna on the Sabbath.

The Hebrews still grumbled. 'There is no water to drink here,' they complained when they camped at Rephidim. 'Why did you bring us out of Egypt to die of thirst?'

Moses cried out to God for help. God told Moses what to do. He walked ahead of the people with some of the leaders to Horeb. He struck a rock with his staff and out poured plenty of water for all the people.

How kind and patient God was with the Hebrews. He is the same today – showing grace and mercy to all who trust in him. The Lord Jesus is described as a rock. From him comes all that we need to satisfy us.

Three months after they left Egypt, Moses and the people (about 600,000 men plus women and children) reached the desert of Sinai. They set up camp and Moses climbed Mount Sinai. God spoke to Moses there.

God gave Moses the important Ten Commandments. These instructed the people then, and us today, about God and how he is to be worshipped and how we ought to treat other people.

God's special agreement or covenant with the people included many other laws. The people solemnly agreed to obey all God's commands.

God called Moses up Mount Sinai again. A thick cloud covered the mountain for sixty days. On the seventh day Moses went into the thick cloud. For forty days and nights the people did not see Moses. They became impatient, thinking that Moses would never come back.

'Make us a golden idol to worship,' they demanded. Sadly, Aaron agreed. He made a golden calf from melted down jewellery. They held a special feast to the Lord and meant to worship God with this golden statue in front of them. They had already forgotten God's command not to make any idols.

God knew what Aaron and the people had done. He was angry with their disobedience. God told Moses what was happening. Moses set off down the mountain carrying two stone tablets on which God had written his laws.

As he came near the camp Moses heard singing. He saw the golden calf and the people dancing round it. Moses was so angry, he hurled the stone tablets to the ground, smashing them.

Moses returned to meet with God, humbly confessing the people's sins to God. God punished their sin but he heard Moses' prayer for mercy and forgiveness. 'My presence will go with you,' God said, 'and I will give you rest.'

God told Moses to cut out two more stone tablets. God wrote his Commandments on them once more.

Moses and the Hebrews wandered in the desert for forty years and had many adventures. God led them with a pillar of cloud by day and a pillar of fire by night. When the pillar moved they knew that it was time to move on.

One time they rebelled against God so badly, he sent serpents into the camp. Many people were bitten. When they realised how wrong they had been, they begged Moses to ask God to take the poisonous snakes away.

God told Moses to put a brass snake on a pole in the camp. If anyone who had been bitten, looked at the brass snake, they would be cured of their sickness. The only way to be cured from the poison of sin is to look in faith to the Lord Jesus Christ who was crucified on the cross to pay the price of sin for those who trust him and love him.

Moses was a man of faith in God. He opposed the evil Pharaoh, and led his people out of slavery in Egypt.

God was faithful and forgave the people again and again. The faithful God forgives sin still because he sent his Son, Jesus Christ, to the world to live and die for his people.